PIANO • VOCAL • GUITAR

90's COUNTRY GOLD

ISBN 0-7935-2106-8

Hal Leonard Publishing Corporation

7777 West Bluemound Road P.O. Box 13819 Milwaukee, WI 53213

ACHY BREAKY HEART
(a.k.a. DON'T TELL MY HEART)

Words and Music by
DON VON TRESS

what a fool I've been and laugh and joke a-bout me on the
fist can tell my lip. He nev-er real-ly liked me an-y-

A

phone.___ You can tell my arms go
way.___ Or tell your Aunt Lou-ise. Tell

back ___ to the farm. ___ You can tell my feet to hit the
an-y-thing you please.___ My-self al-read-y knows I'm not o-

E

floor. Or you can tell my lips to
kay. Or you can tell my eyes to

5

Don't tell my heart, my ach-y break-y heart._ I just don't think he'd un-der-

stand. And if you tell my heart, my ach-y break-y heart,_ he

might blow_ up and kill this man. Ooh._

ANYMORE

Words and Music by TRAVIS TRITT
and JILL COLUCCI

BROTHERLY LOVE

Words and Music by JIMMY STEWART
and TIM NICHOLS

Easy Country two-beat

We share the same __ last name __
You hat-ed girls __ 'til I __
They share the same __ last name __

__ and the same __ col-or eyes, __
__ had my __ first _____ date. __
__ and the same __ col-or eyes, __

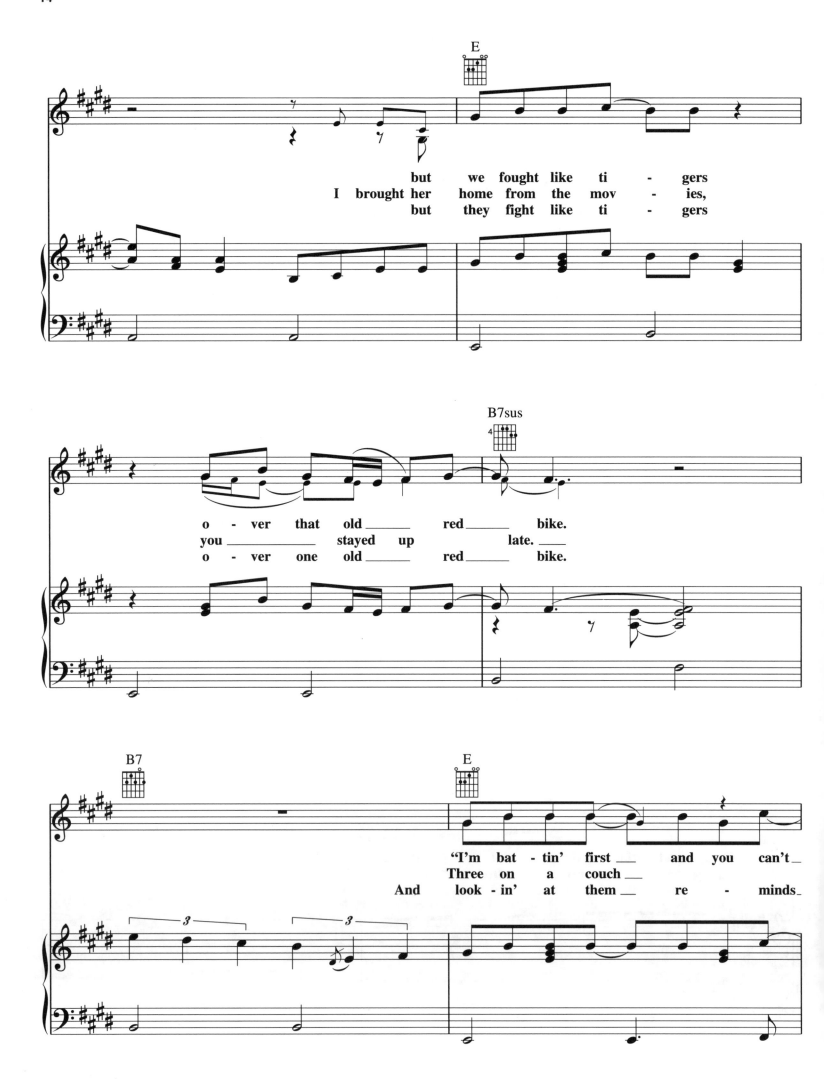

18

BOOT SCOOTIN' BOOGIE

Words and Music by
RONNIE DUNN

COME IN OUT OF THE PAIN

Words and Music by FRANK J. MYERS
and DON PFRIMMER

DOWN AT THE TWIST AND SHOUT

Words and Music by
MARY-CHAPIN CARPENTER

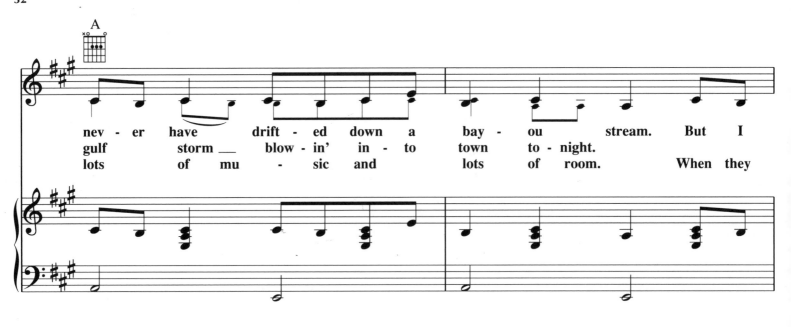

never have drift - ed down a bay - ou stream. But I
gulf storm ___ blow - in' in - to town to - night.
lots of mu - sic and lots of room. When they

heard that mu - sic on the ra - di - o, and I ___
Liv - in' on the del - ta it's quite ___ a show. ___ They got hur -
play you a waltz from a nine - teen ten, you're

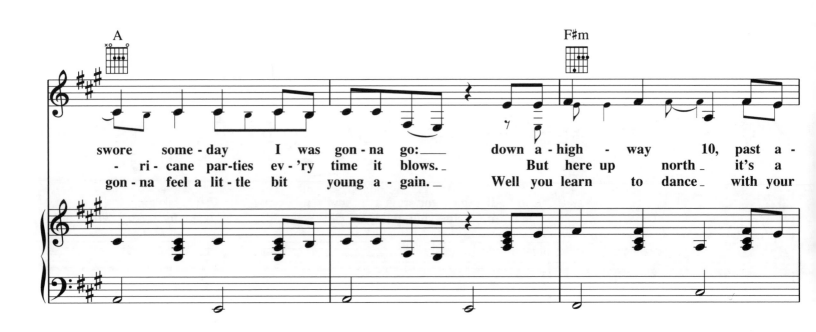

swore some - day I was gon - na go: ___ down a high - way 10, past a-
- ri - cane par-ties ev - 'ry time it blows. ___ But here up north ___ it's a
gon - na feel a lit - tle bit young a - gain. ___ Well you learn to dance ___ with your

THE GREATEST MAN I NEVER KNEW

Words and Music by RICHARD LEIGH
and LAYNG MARTINE, JR.

The great-est man I_____ nev - er knew_____ lived just down the hall,_____
The great-est man I_____ nev - er knew_____ came home late ev - 'ry night,_____
The great-est words I_____ nev - er heard_____ I guess I'll nev - er hear._____

EVEN THE MAN IN
THE MOON IS CRYIN'

Words and Music by DON COOK
and MARK COLLIE

FRIENDS IN LOW PLACES

Words and Music by DEWAYNE BLACKWELL
and EARL BUD LEE

48

HERE'S A QUARTER
(CALL SOMEONE WHO CARES)

Words and Music by
TRAVIS TRITT

I FEEL LUCKY

Words and Music by MARY-CHAPIN CARPENTER
and DON SCHLITZ

I'LL THINK OF SOMETHING

Words and Music by JERRY FOSTER
and BILL RICE

IF I KNOW ME

Words and Music by DEAN DILLON
and PAM BELFORD

IF THERE HADN'T BEEN YOU

Words and Music by RON HELLARD
and TOM SHAPIRO

if there had-n't been ___ you ___ on my side, _____

you in ___ my life. _____ All my dreams ____ would still be dreams_

_____ if there had-n't been ___ you. ____

IN A DIFFERENT LIGHT

Words and Music by BUCKY JONES, BOB McDILL
and DICKEY LEE

MEET IN THE MIDDLE

Words and Music by CHAPIN HARTFORD, JIM FOSTER
and DON PFRIMMER

KEEP IT BETWEEN THE LINES

Words and Music by RUSSELL SMITH
and KATHY LOUVIN

Moderate four-beat

He was

sit - tin' be - side___ me in the pas - sen - ger seat as I
sit - tin' in my chair,___ kind - a sneak - in' a look at him
fin - ished the pic - ture and I put him to bed. Got

looked through the wind - shield at the qui - et lit - tle street. He was
ly - in' on the floor___ with his col - or - ing book. Then he
down on my knees___ and I bowed my head. And I said,

LOVE WITHOUT END, AMEN

Words and Music by
AARON G. BARKER

just be - tween____ us." You see,

dad-dy's just__ don't love__ their chil - dren ev - 'ry now__ and then,_____

it's a love with-out end,___ A - men. It's a

love with-out end,___ A - men.

MY NEXT BROKEN HEART

Words and Music by DON COOK,
RONNIE DUNN and KIX BROOKS

100

NEON MOON

Words and Music by
RONNIE DUNN

107

NO ONE ELSE ON EARTH

Words and Music by SAM LORBER,
STEWART HARRIS and JILL COLUCCI

I'm out of con - trol.
and it ain't o - ver yet.

How did you get to me?

No - one else on earth could ev - er hurt me, break my heart the way you do.

No - one else on earth was ev - er worth it.

No - one can love me like, no - one can love me like you.

NOTHING SHORT OF DYING

Words and Music by
TRAVIS TRITT

113

114

'Cause there ain't noth-ing short of dy-ing that's worse than be - ing left _ a -

lone.

lone.

There ain't noth-ing short of dy-ing that's worse than be - ing left _ a -

lone. _____

SACRED GROUND

Words and Music by KIX BROOKS
and VERNON RUST

120

SHE IS HIS ONLY NEED

Words and Music by
DAVE LOGGINS

Bil - ly was small town lon - er __ who nev - er did dream __ of ev - er leav-ing south-ern Ar - i - zo - na __ or ev - er hear-ing wed-ding bells __ ring.

SHAMELESS

Words and Music by
BILLY JOEL

132

SOMEWHERE IN MY BROKEN HEART

Words and Music by BILLY DEAN
and RICHARD LEIGH

135

STRAIGHT TEQUILA NIGHT

Words and Music by DEBBIE HUPP
and KENT ROBBINS

SO MUCH LIKE MY DAD

Words and Music by CHIPS MOMAN
and BOBBY EMMONS

Country Ballad

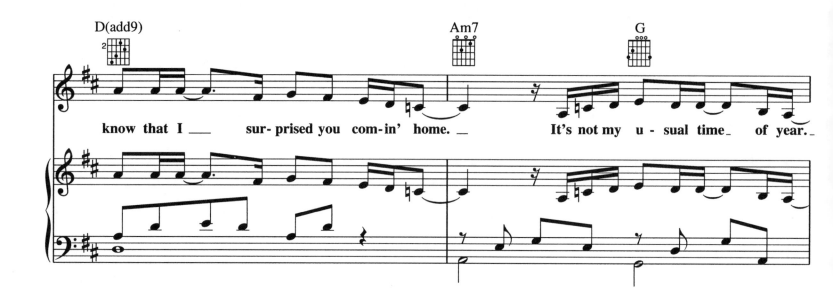

know that I ___ sur-prised you com-in' home. ___ It's not my u-sual time ___ of year. ___

But I've got my-self a prob-lem and I know ___

144

said that al-ways made you __ stay.

She says she's gon-na

Repeat ad lib. and Fade

YOU KNOW ME BETTER THAN THAT

By TONY HASELDEN
and ANNA LISA GRAHAM

Ba - by, since you left ___ me ___ there's some - bod - y new. ___
pic - nics and blue ___ jeans ___ and buck - ets of beer, ___ now it's

She thinks I'm per - fect, I swear. ___
bal - let and sym - pho - ny hall. ___

Your Favorites in COUNTRY MUSIC *and more...*

#1 COUNTRY SONGS OF THE 80'S
44 Chart-topping country hits, including: American Made • Any Day Now • Could I Have This Dance • Crying My Heart Out Over You • Forever And Ever Amen • Forty Hour Week (For A Livin') • Grandpa (Tell Me 'Bout The Good Old Days) • He Stopped Loving Her Today • I Was In The Stream • My Heroes Have Always Been Cowboys • Smoky Mountain Rain • Why Not Me • You're The Reason God Made Oklahoma.
_____00360715 $12.95

80'S LADIES—TOP HITS FROM COUNTRY WOMEN OF THE 80'S
23 songs by today's female country stars including: Roseanne Cash, Crystal Gayle, The Judds, Reba McEntire, Anne Murray, K.T. Oslin and others. Songs include: I Don't Know Why You Don't Want Me • Lyin' In His Arms Again • Why Not Me • A Sunday Kind Of Love • Could I Have This Dance • Do'Ya • Strong Enough To Bend.
_____00359741 $9.95

THE AWARD-WINNING SONGS OF THE COUNTRY MUSIC ASSOCIATION First Edition
All of the official top five songs nominated for the CMA "Song Of The Year" from 1967 to 1983. 85 selections, featuring: Always On My Mind • Behind Closed Doors • Don't It Make My Brown Eyes Blue • Elvira • The Gambler • I.O.U. • Mammas Don't Let Your Babies Grow Up To Be Cowboys • Swingin' • You're The Reason God Made Oklahoma.
_____00359485 $16.95

AWARD WINNING SONGS OF THE COUNTRY MUSIC ASSOCIATION Second Edition
An update to the first edition, this songbook features 18 songs nominated for "Song of the Year" by the Country Music Association from 1984 through 1991. Songs include: Islands In The Stream • Chiseled In Stone • Don't Rock The Jukebox • Friends In Low Places • God Bless The U.S.A. • Grandpa (Tell Me 'Bout The Good Old Days) • All My Ex's Live In Texas • Forever And Ever, Amen.
_____00359486 $8.95

THE NEW ULTIMATE COUNTRY FAKE BOOK
More than 700 of the greatest country hits of all-time. Includes an alphabetical index and an artist index! Includes: Cold, Cold Heart • Crazy • Crying My Heart Out Over You • Daddy Sang Bass • Diggin' Up Bones • God Bless The U.S.A. • Grandpa (Tell Me 'Bout The Good Old Days) • Great Balls Of Fire • Green, Green Grass Of Home • He Stopped Loving Her Today • I.O.U. • I Was Country When Country Wasn't Cool • I Wouldn't Have Missed It For The World • Lucille • Mammas Don't Let Your Babies Grow Up To Be Cowboys • On The Other Hand • Ruby, Don't Take Your Love To Town • Swingin' • Talking In Your Sleep • Through The Years • Whoever's In New England • Why Not Me • You Needed Me • and MORE!
_____00240049 $35.00

THE BEST COUNTRY SONGS EVER
We've updated this outstanding collection of country songs to include even more of your favorites—over 75 in all! Featuring: Always On My Mind • Behind Closed Doors • Could I Have This Dance • Crazy • Daddy Sang Bass • D-I-V-O-R-C-E • Forever And Ever, Amen • God Bless The U.S.A. • Grandpa (Tell Me 'Bout The Good Old Days) • Help Me Make It Through The Night • I Fall To Pieces • If We Make It Through December • Jambalaya (On The Bayou) • Love Without End, Amen • Mammas Don't Let Your Babies Grow Up To Be Cowboys • Stand By Your Man • Through The Years • and more. Features stay-open binding.
_____00359135 $16.95

THE GREAT AMERICAN COUNTRY SONGBOOK
The absolute best collection of top country songs anywhere. 70 titles, featuring: Any Day Now • Could I Have This Dance • Heartbroke • I Was Country When Country Wasn't Cool • I'm Gonna Hire A Wino To Decorate Our Home • It's Hard To Be Humble • Jambalaya • Smokey Mountain Rain • Through The Years • many others.
_____00359947 $12.95

COUNTRY LOVE SONGS
25 Sentimental country favorites, including: Could I Have This Dance • Forever And Ever, Amen • She Believes In Me • Through The Years • The Vows Go Unbroken • You Decorated My Life • You Needed Me • and more.
_____00311528 $9.95

51 COUNTRY STANDARDS
A collection of 51 of country's biggest hits, including: (Hey Won't You Play) Another Somebody Done Somebody Wrong Song • By The Time I Get To Phoenix • Could I Have This Dance • Daddy Sang Bass • Forever And Ever, Amen • Bless The U.S.A. • Green, Green Grass Of Home • Islands In The Stream • King Of The Road • Little Green Apples • Lucille • Mammas Don't Let Your Babies Grow Up To Be Cowboys • Ruby Don't Take Your Love To Town • Stand By Me • Through The Years • Your Cheatin' Heart.
_____00359517 $10.95

COUNTRY MUSIC HALL OF FAME
The Country Music Hall Of Fame Was Founded in 1961 by the Country Music Association (CMA). Each Year, new members are elected—and these books are the first to represent all of its members with photos, biography and music selections related to each individual.

Volume 1
Includes: Fred Rose, Hank Williams, Jimmie Rodgers, Roy Acuff, George D. Hay, PeeWee King, Minnie Pearl and Grandpa Jones. 23 songs, including: Blue Eyes Crying In The Rain • Cold, Cold Heart • Wabash Cannon Ball • Tennesse Waltz.
_____00359510 $8.95

Volume 2
Features: Tex Ritter, Ernest Tubb, Eddy Arnold, Jim Denny, Joseph Lee Frank, Uncle Dave Macon, Jim Reeves and Bill Monroe. Songs include: Jealous Heart • Walking The Floor Over You • Make The World Go Away • Ruby, Don't Take Your Love To Town • Kentucky Waltz • Is It Really Over • many more.
_____00359504 $8.95

Volume 3
Red Foley, Steve Sholes, Bob Wills, Gene Autry, Original Carter Family, Arthur Satherley, Jimmie Davis, and The Orginal Sons Of The Pioneers. 24 songs: Peace In The Valley • Ashes Of Love • San Antonio Rose • Tumbling Tumble Weeds • Born To Lose • Worried Man's Blues • many more.
_____00359508 $8.95

Volume 4
Features: Chet Atkins, Patsy Cline, Owen Bradley, Kitty Wells, Hank Snow, Hubert Long, Connie B. Gay and Lefty Frizzell. Song highlights: Crazy • I'm Sorry • Making Believe • Wings Of A Dove • Saginaw, Michigan • and 16 others.
_____00359509 $8.95

Volume 5
Includes: Merle Travis, Johnny Cash, Grant Turner, Vernon Dalhart, Marty Robbins, Roy Horton, "Little" Jimmie Dickens. 19 selections: Sixteen Tons • Folsom Prison Blues • El Paso • Mockingbird Hill • May The Bird of Paradise.
_____00359512 $8.95

019